William Bolcom

Le Fantôme du Clavecin

for Harpsichord

Edited by Davitt Moroney

ISBN 978-1-4768-1851-1

EDWARD B. MARKS MUSIC COMPANY

Exclusively Distributed By

HAL•LEONARD® CORPORATION

7777 W. BLUEMOUND RD. P.O. BOX 13819 MILWAUKEE, WI 53213

www.ebmarks.com
www.halleonard.com

This work is conceived for a French-style harpsichord with two manuals, which are coupled by pushing in the upper keyboard, and with a range from 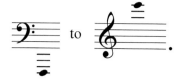 to 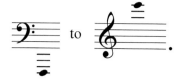.

It is possible to play this with an equal-tempered tuning, but a French-style temperament from the time of François Couperin, with its more piquant intervals, will give extra tang to the sound and make it possible to program *Le Fantôme du Clavecin* with Couperin or other French music of around his time. (Indeed the whole of *Le Fantôme* is conceived with the Couperin *ordres* very much in mind.) Unlike the *ordres*, which are each in one key (or its parallel), *Le Fantôme* exploits the *mi contra fa* diabolical conflict, which is the source of the tonal and stylistic imbalance throughout this *"désordre."*

The following manual indications are only suggestions:
Ⓘ = lower manual (uncoupled), Ⓘ = upper manual (not always specified); Ⓘ+Ⅱ = the two coupled and played on Ⓘ.

ORNAMENTS are to be played in the 18th-century convention of taking value from the following note, including slashed gracenotes (written thus for differentiation). The table resembles Couperin's in most respects:

Ordinary trill: 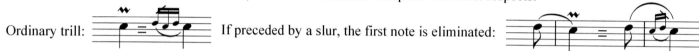 If preceded by a slur, the first note is eliminated:

(All other trills start on top note.)

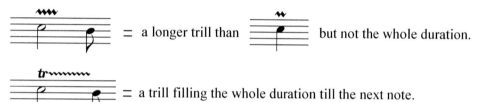 = a longer trill than but not the whole duration.

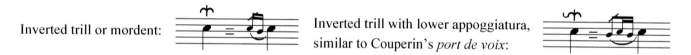 = a trill filling the whole duration till the next note.

Inverted trill or mordent: 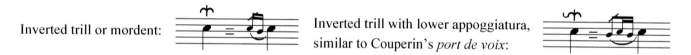 Inverted trill with lower appoggiatura, similar to Couperin's *port de voix*:

 = a turn.

 = a turn followed by a trill.

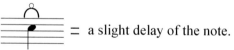 = a slight delay of the note.

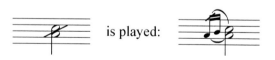 is played:

The "Sarabande des Profondeurs" is written in the "white" notation common in Couperin's time:

Players are not only allowed but encouraged to modify ornaments on repeats, within traditional ornamental conventions.

ACCIDENTALS: In music with key signatures, traditional rules apply. In music without key signatures, accidentals obtain throughout a beamed group. Unbeamed notes within a measure continue the same accidental until interrupted by another note or rest. (Additional courtesy accidentals are given to ensure clarity.)

—William Bolcom

for Davitt Moroney
World Premiere by Andreas Skouras at the Handel House Museum, London, UK on May 11, 2010

Le Fantôme du Clavecin
for harpsichord

I. Prélude: Le Monstre Souterrain.

WILLIAM BOLCOM
(2005)

Very free; senza tempo

A little faster

contemplative, very free; fairly slow

* two slashes through stem: a very short gracenote

II. L'Allemande Hargneuse.

Majestueux ♩ = 42

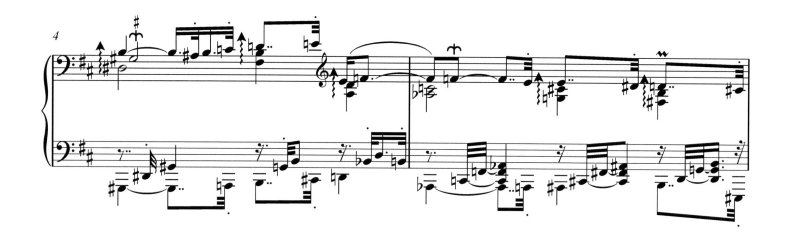

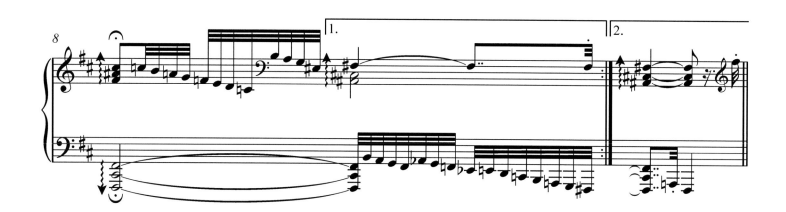

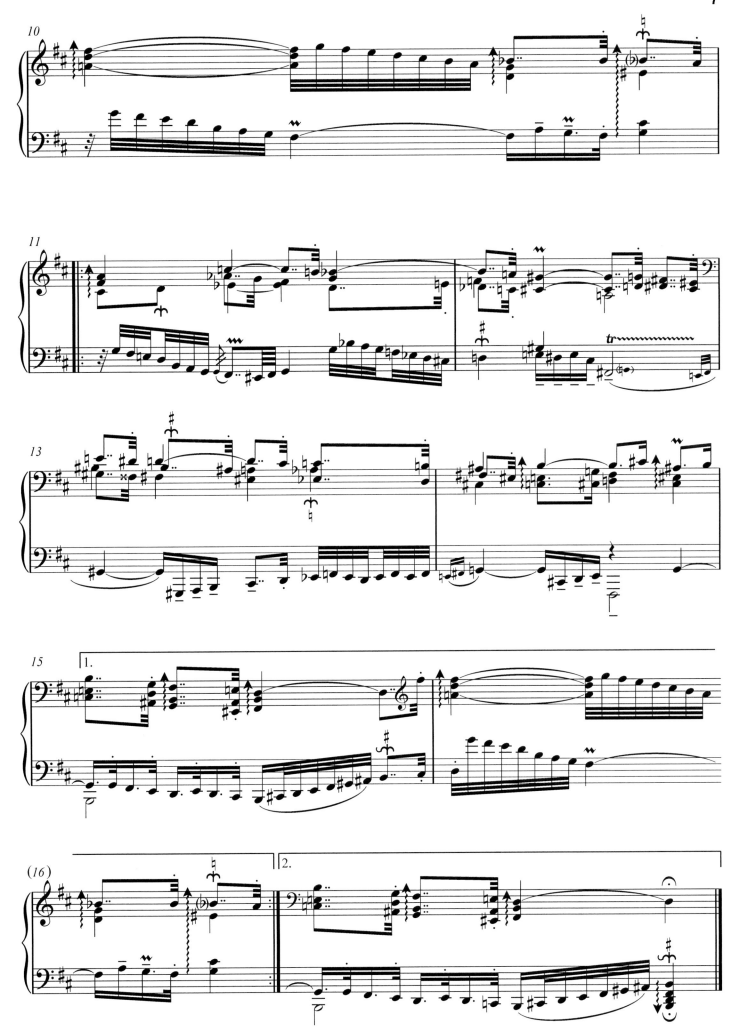

8

III. La Pucelle-Cantatrice.

Gracieusement, chantant; très intime

molto legato

notes inégales

Plus lent

rit.

IV. Courante des Souris de l'Opéra *(Pièce Croisée)*

Vivement; très léger ♩ = c.76

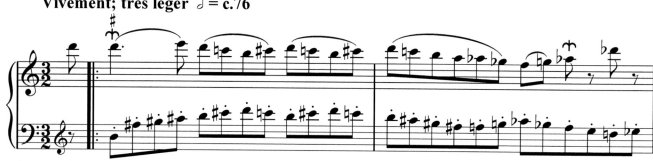

2 manuals, uncoupled; *notes égales*

V. L'Insouciant.

Lively ♩ = 72

notes inégales

1. Da Capo
2. continue
3. to Le Soucieux
4. to L'Enragé
5. to Coda

Le Soucieux. (1° Couplet)

3. L'istesso tempo

*legato r.h.,
notes égales*

Bourdon

L'Enragé (2° Couplet)

Coda

notes inégales

rit.

Blank for page turn

VI. L'Air du Temps Perdu.

Stately ♩ = c.60; *lyrical, with a swing (between ♪♪ and ♪⸱♪)*

VII. Danse des Critiques.

En pointe ♩. = 56

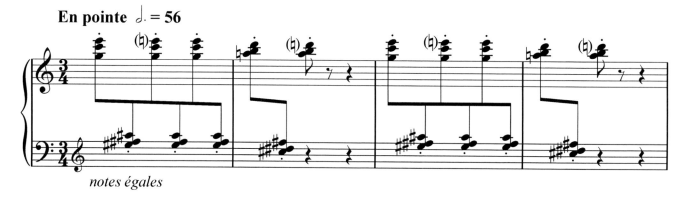

notes égales

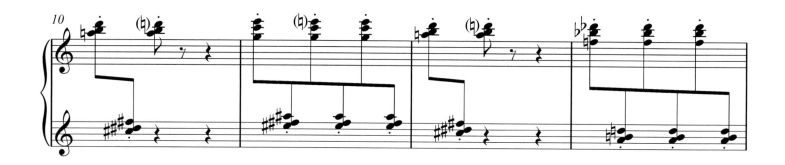

1° Couplet

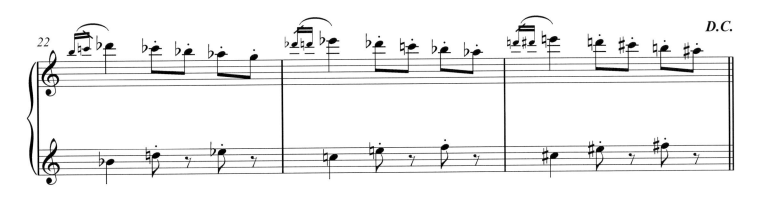

2° Couplet

VIII. Sarabande des Profondeurs.

Gravement, très lent

Pour finir; un peu plus lent

IX. La Gigue-Bataille.

Très vite (♩. = 72)